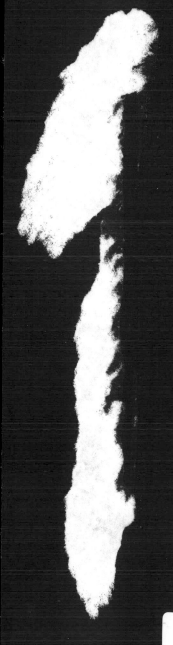

PUFFIN BOOKS

UK | USA | Canada | Ireland | Australia
India | New Zealand | South Africa

Puffin Books is part of the Penguin Random House group of companies whose
addresses can be found at global.penguinrandomhouse.com.

puffinbooks.com

Penguin
Random House
UK

First published 2015
001

Text and illustrations copyright © Mind Candy, 2015
Written by Steve Cleverley

Printed in Slovakia

A CIP catalogue record for this book is available from the British Library

ISBN: 978–0–141–36033–1

World of WARRIORS

BOOK OF WARRIORS

PUFFIN

CONTENTS

IN THE WILDLANDS, ONLY THE BRAVEST SURVIVE!

History's greatest warriors have been summoned through time to the mysterious Wildlands, where they must defeat King Boneshaker's deadly Skull Army. Now, you can follow in their footsteps.

Take a journey through the toughest eras in history to discover what makes these fearsome fighters tick. Which daring Trojan fell for a devious wooden horse trick? Which furious Viking maiden made mincemeat of her shipmates? And who ended up in the Wildlands after plummeting from a crumbling tower?

The answers to all of these questions and many more lie inside . . . the Book of Warriors!

KEY:

YEAR SUMMONED:
The year the warrior was
plucked from history
to do battle!

YEAR:
103 BC

SPECIAL MOVE:
The symbol of the
warrior's special move.

ELEMENT:
All warriors belong
to one of the four
elements: Water, Air,
Fire or Earth.

MAP:
Where in the world
the warrior
hails from.

AGE OF
DISCOVERY

9. MUNGO

7. SPURIUS

8. HANNIBAL

1. **UNK** THE STONE-AGE SAVAGE
   10,000 BC, STONE AGE EUROPE

2. **SAMA** THE MINOAN WARRIOR
   1700 BC, MINOA

3. **RAM** THE EGYPTIAN WARRIOR
   1330 BC, ANCIENT EGYPT

4. **YADA** THE FEROCIOUS PHOENICIAN
   965 BC, PHOENICIA

5. **BADDA** THE PERSIAN IMMORTAL
   539 BC, ACHAEMENID EMPIRE

6. **PELION** THE SPARTAN WARRIOR
   480 BC, SPARTA

7. **SPURIUS** THE ETRUSCAN WARRIOR
   351 BC, ETURIA

8. **HANNIBAL** THE CARTHAGINIAN GENERAL
   218 BC, CARTHAGE

9. **MUNGO** THE CELTIC BERSERKER
   218 BC, ANCIENT BRITAIN

10. **WANG** THE HAN WARRIOR
    202 BC, HAN DYNASTY CHINA

1. UNK

6. PELION

2. SAMA

10. WANG

5. BADDA

4. YADA

3. RAM

N
W · E
S

UNK
THE STONE AGE SAVAGE

Having gained a fearsome reputation thanks to the innovative way he dismembered rival tribesmen with his teeth, Unk was enjoying life as the main man in his settlement. But events took a strange turn when he was summoned to the Wildlands while skinning a wolf, and now he's seriously angry!

ELEMENT:	FIRE
LIKES:	MURALS
DISLIKES:	CLOTHING
WEAPON:	CLUB

SPECIAL MOVE:
BERSERK – Drains some health and attacks opponents.

FIGHTING FACTS

Stone Age warriors with headaches had holes drilled in their skulls, and most survived. Beats painkillers!

SUPER RARE

UTU
THE SUMERIAN WARRIOR

Patrolling the walled city of Uruk after dark, Utu was set upon by thugs who demanded his ceremonial dagger. Keen to rip them limb from limb, this valiant warrior began lashing out in fury but quickly found himself slicing through shadows as he was summoned, mid-brawl, to the Wildlands.

ELEMENT: AIR
LIKES: GIFTS FROM GILGAMESH
DISLIKES: FILTHY THIEVES
WEAPON: SHORT SWORD
SPECIAL MOVE: AIR BOOST — Temporarily increases air damage inflicted by all team members.

FIGHTING FACTS

Sumerians prized their property extremely highly, so thieves were tortured and dismembered. Brutal, but effective!

LEGENDARY

LABASHI
THE AKKADIAN WARRIOR

Labashi is convinced he was summoned to the Wildlands after being cursed by a sorceress who accused him of stealing her bracelet. But it is most likely due to him being one of the Akkadian Empire's most fearless warriors. Then again, he does love stealing bracelets!

ELEMENT: AIR
LIKES: PILFERING GOLD
DISLIKES: ANCIENT CURSES
WEAPON: SWORD
SPECIAL MOVE: AIR BOOST —
temporarily increase air damage inflicted by all team members.

FIGHTING FACTS

Akkadian warriors were amongst the first to use the composite bow. Three times as powerful as a normal bow, it could puncture early armour from considerable distances.

SUPER RARE

SAMA
THE MINOAN WARRIOR

Returning to the Palace of Knossos after a highly successful boar hunt, Sama spotted what looked like a man with huge horns running into the abandoned labyrinth. Curious, this hot-headed warrior gave chase but became lost in the vast maze, finally emerging in the Wildlands, disorientated and enraged.

ELEMENT: AIR
LIKES: BULL LEAPING
DISLIKES: LABYRINTHS
WEAPON: SWORD
SPECIAL MOVE: PHANTOM SHIELD – Boosts the Armour strength of all team members!

FIGHTING FACTS

Minoans enjoyed bull leaping, a ritual that saw them grabbing a bull's horns, causing it to jerk its neck and propel them into the air.

LEGENDARY

RARE

KUSOS
THE MYCENAEAN WARRIOR

Filthy rich thanks to the jewels he pilfered during the conquest of Crete, Kusos was planning to desert and retire to Asia Minor. But this conniving warrior's plans came to an abrupt end when he was summoned to the Wildlands while protecting his pet rat from Minoan thugs.

ELEMENT: FIRE
LIKES: STOLEN GEMS
DISLIKES: HONESTY
WEAPON: AXE

SPECIAL MOVE:
FIRE STORM — Burn all enemies with FIRE power as the fight progresses.

FIGHTING FACTS

With helmets made from boars' tusks and protective plates made of bronze, Mycenaean armour was so cumbersome it could only be worn by warriors riding in chariots.

COMMON

18

RAM
THE EGYPTIAN WARRIOR

YEAR: 1330 BC

Lost in a fierce sandstorm after falling from his chariot during a skirmish with some Nubians, Ram was attempting to reach the Nile when he came across what looked like a plundered tomb. Taking shelter, he fell asleep, only to wake up in the Wildlands.

ELEMENT: WATER
LIKES: SPARRING WITH SLAVES
DISLIKES: SANDSTORMS
WEAPON: KHOPESH

SPECIAL MOVE:
POISON — Drain your enemy's energy slowly as the fight progresses.

FIGHTING FACTS

Cats were sacred in Ancient Egypt, so the Persians would hold up live ones (and even pictures of them) during battle to stop the Egyptians from firing arrows at them. Meow!

TARHU

THE HITTITE WARRIOR

YEAR:
1274 BC

As arrows rained down and thousands of chariots led by Ramses II thundered into view, Tarhu raced towards the Fortress of Kadesh, convinced he would soon meet his maker. But a mysterious old man suddenly grabbed his hand, and this daring Hittite found himself in the Wildlands.

ELEMENT:	EARTH	**SPECIAL MOVE:**
LIKES:	COLLECTING SEVERED HANDS	POISON HIVE — Drain
DISLIKES:	SURRENDER	all enemies slowly
WEAPON:	XIPHOS	with poison.

FIGHTING FACTS

The Hittites used war chariots as all-out assault weapons to crash through lines of enemy infantry. The result? Total, limb smashing carnage!

RARE

HECTOR
THE TROJAN WARRIOR

Hector was the greatest swordsman in all of Troy, but even he fell for the Greeks' devious wooden horse trick. In fact, he was about to be crushed beneath its wheels when he was knocked sideways by a boulder flung from a trebuchet — only to wake up in the Wildlands.

ELEMENT: FIRE
LIKES: THE CLASH OF SWORDS
DISLIKES: SOOTHSAYERS
WEAPON: KOPIS
SPECIAL MOVE: FIRE STORM — Burn all enemies with FIRE power as the fight progresses.

FIGHTING FACTS

As their city burned, some Trojan Warriors put on enemy armour pilfered from fallen opponents and launched sneaky counter-attacks.

LEGENDARY

YADA
THE FEROCIOUS PHOENICIAN

Hand-picked to guard a precious cargo en route to Carthage, Yada was below decks honing his sword when he heard screaming. Storming outside, he faced a scene of utter carnage — but was summoned to the Wildlands before he could attack the murderous mutineers led by the ship's cook.

ELEMENT:	WATER	**SPECIAL MOVE:**
LIKES:	THE COLOUR PURPLE	THUNDER STRIKE —
DISLIKES:	LONG VOYAGES	Electrocute the enemy with
WEAPON:	KOPIS	the power of lightning.

FIGHTING FACTS

The prized purple dye made famous by the Phoenicians was derived from the mucus of a sea snail called the murex. Yuck!

COMMON

23

RARE

ZUU
THE BABYLONIAN WARRIOR

YEAR:
600 BC

Fighting off traitors as he dangled from the vines of the Hanging Gardens of Babylon, Zuu tried to make his escape by leaping into the raging Euphrates River. Unfortunately, this daring warrior was summoned to the Wildlands mid-leap, and now spends every day wondering what became of his king, Nebuchadnezzar II.

ELEMENT: EARTH
LIKES: HORTICULTURE
DISLIKES: GREENFLY
WEAPON: SWORD

SPECIAL MOVE:
BOULDER BASH — Crush all enemies with EARTH power.

FIGHTING FACTS

King Nebuchadnezzar II was said to have been afflicted by a madness that made him think he was a wild beast.

25

BADDA
THE PERSIAN IMMORTAL

Having dropped his trusty sword in the River Tigris during the Battle of Opis, Badda was forced to fight off several Babylonians with his bare hands. Injured, he found sanctuary in a destroyed temple but was summoned to the Wildlands the second he stepped on a glowing talisman.

ELEMENT: EARTH
LIKES: ELABORATE ROBES
DISLIKES: INELEGANT FIGHTING
WEAPON: SHAMSHIR
SPECIAL MOVE: EARTH BOOST — Boosts EARTH damage inflicted by all team members.

FIGHTING FACTS

Elite Immortals were so called because dead and wounded warriors were instantaneously replaced, giving the impression that they were indeed immortal.

LEGENDARY

PELION
THE SPARTAN WARRIOR

Surrounded by Persian invaders,
Pelion was fighting alongside
King Leonidas when he suddenly
remembered something the
Oracle of Delphi had said to him about
a mysterious world of warriors. But
just as he was warning the king about
the Oracle's strange prediction, he was
summoned to the Wildlands.

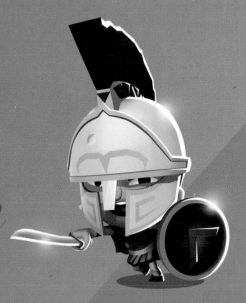

ELEMENT: FIRE
LIKES: BODY OIL
DISLIKES: CRYPTIC PROPHECIES
WEAPON: KOPIS
SPECIAL MOVE: BOMBARD – Calls a delayed
air strike on whichever opponent is on screen.

FIGHTING FACTS

Trainee Spartan soldiers were
encouraged to kill a slave as
part of their training.

SUPER RARE

SPURIUS
THE ETRUSCAN WARRIOR

Visiting the Bay of Naples for peace talks, Spurius was planning to slay as many Roman negotiators as possible the second things turned sour. But the talks went surprisingly well and this bloodthirsty warrior was summoned to the Wildlands while chopping only his eighth envoy to bits.

ELEMENT:	EARTH
LIKES:	DOUBLE CROSSES
DISLIKES:	PEACE
WEAPON:	XIPHOS
SPECIAL MOVE:	EARTH BOOST –

Boosts EARTH damage inflicted by all team members.

FIGHTING FACTS

Some Etruscan helmets featured cutaway sections over the ears so that warriors could hear the formation signals given by war trumpets.

LEGENDARY

HELIOS
THE MACEDONIAN WARRIOR

Helios never did find out who won the Battle of the Persian Gate. Trapped on a narrow mountain pass as Persian forces rained down boulders, this tactical genius had just devised a brilliant pincer attack when he slipped into an icy ravine and found himself in the Wildlands.

ELEMENT: AIR
LIKES: PHILOSOPHY
DISLIKES: ASSASSINATION PLOTS
WEAPON: KOPIS
SPECIAL MOVE: TEAM STRIKE — Draws health from entire team to strike enemies.

FIGHTING FACTS

Crazy Roman Emperor Caligula dug up Alexander the Great's body and stole the Macedonian hero's armour so he could wear it himself!

LEGENDARY

29

ISAK
THE NUBIAN HUNTER

Lurking behind a sand dune by the Nile, Isak was preparing to sneak aboard a Roman barge when he was distracted by a huge shimmering pyramid that appeared from nowhere. As he ran to investigate, the mysterious structure vanished and Isak was whisked to the Wildlands.

ELEMENT: FIRE
LIKES: GOLD JEWELLERY
DISLIKES: CROCODILES
WEAPON: SHOTEL SWORD
SPECIAL MOVE: POISON HIVE —
Drain all enemies slowly with poison.

FIGHTING FACTS

With its curved, sickle-like blade, the shotel sword was ideal for hooking enemy warriors right off their horses.

SUPER RARE

CLOVIS
THE FRANKISH WARRIOR

Wanted for murder, this degenerate Frankish brute was on the run in the Rhine valley when he hooked up with a band of pirates. Eager to impress, Clovis was ransacking a Roman supply ship when he was suddenly summoned to the Wildlands, still brandishing a stolen bottle of wine.

ELEMENT: WATER
LIKES: MURDER MOST FOUL
DISLIKES: HARD WORK
WEAPON: LONG SEAX

SPECIAL MOVE:
HEALING — Restore health to all team members.

FIGHTING FACTS

The Frankish javelin featured barbs designed to puncture flesh and hold the weapon in place, making its removal excruciatingly painful and invariably lethal.

COMMON

COMMON

KENDRIX
THE CELTIC WARRIOR

Wading through a sodden ditch while scouting an enemy hill fort after dark, Kendrix found himself surrounded by torch-wielding druids. Deciding that death was preferable to surrender, this reckless barbarian rushed at his foes but was summoned to the Wildlands the second he raised his long sword.

ELEMENT: AIR
LIKES: TURNIPS
DISLIKES: DRUIDS
WEAPON: LONG SWORD

SPECIAL MOVE:
BERSERK — Drains some health and attacks opponents.

FIGHTING FACTS

As well as decorating their homes with severed heads, some Celtic warriors collected enemy brains and wore them on their belts.

HANNIBAL
THE CARTHAGINIAN GENERAL

A military genius, Hannibal was crossing the Alps during the Second Punic War when a rockfall halted his progress. Ingenious as ever, he attempted to fracture the boulders using vinegar and fire, but something went wrong and he was summoned to the Wildlands in a flash of vinegary blue light!

ELEMENT:	AIR	
LIKES:	MOBILIZING ARMIES	
DISLIKES:	VINEGAR AND FIRE	
WEAPON:	FALCATA	

SPECIAL MOVE:
BOMBARD — Calls a delayed air strike on whichever opponent is on screen.

FIGHTING FACTS

It is estimated that Hannibal mobilized up to 100,000 troops and thirty-seven elephants for his Alpine crossing to Rome.

RARE

35

MUNGO
THE CELTIC BERSERKER

Mad, blue and barbarous to know, Mungo is famed for his frenzied attacks on Roman settlements. But one thing this crazed Celt hates more than Romans is the fact he was summoned to the Wildlands while riding a war elephant across the Alps with his hero Hannibal.

ELEMENT: WATER
LIKES: RAMPANT VIOLENCE
DISLIKES: ROMANS
WEAPON: LONG SWORD
SPECIAL MOVE: BERSERK — This powerful attack will drain some of your own health!

FIGHTING FACTS

Celtic warriors often served as mercenaries and painted themselves blue to terrify enemies. Some even spiked and lime-washed their hair before battle.

LEGENDARY

WANG
THE HAN WARRIOR

Wang was eating noodles on the outskirts of the Gobi Desert when a flying dagger struck his commander. Pursuing the fleeing assassin across the rooftops, this heroic warrior fell into a laundry basket, which then tumbled down a hill and somehow came to a halt in the Wildlands.

ELEMENT: EARTH
LIKES: EXTRACTING INFORMATION
DISLIKES: DIRTY LAUNDRY
WEAPON: SWORD
SPECIAL MOVE: VENGEANCE —
Attack power rises as health reduces.

FIGHTING FACTS

Kites were invented during the Han period and were used by the military to send messages, scare the enemy, and measure distance and wind direction.

RARE

AGE OF SWORDS

1. **WULF** THE HARII BRUTE
   10 AD, BELGICA

2. **CRIXUS** THE ROMAN GLADIATOR
   112 AD, ANCIENT ROME

3. **ANIL** THE GUPTA WARRIOR
   380 AD, GUPTA EMPIRE

4. **GOAR** THE ALANS WARRIOR
   426 AD, LUSITANIA

5. **HUNERIC** THE VANDAL KING
   484 AD, ANCIENT NORTH AFRICA

6. **PACORUS** THE PARTHIAN WARRIOR
   58 AD, PARTHIAN EMPIRE

7. **SENI** THE MEROITIC WARRIOR
   61 AD, MEROE

8. **ERIKA** THE VIKING SHIELD MAIDEN
   621 AD, MEDIEVAL SCANDINAVIA

9. **PING** THE TANG DYNASTY PRINCESS
   623 AD, TANG DYNASTY CHINA

10. **BRETH** THE PICT WARRIOR
    685 AD, FORTIU

10. BRETH

2. CRIXUS

5. HUNERIC

8. ERIKA

1. WULF

4. GOAR

9. PING

6. PACORUS

7. SENI

3. ANIL

N
W E
S

YEAR:
65 BC

JUBA
THE NUMIDIAN GLADIATOR

Snatched from his African homeland and forced to fight alongside condemned criminals in the elaborate funeral games held for Caesar's father, Juba was fending off a crazed rhino when he tumbled through a trapdoor and found himself in the Wildlands, with the unfortunate creature's severed horn jammed in his rump.

ELEMENT: EARTH
LIKES: PUMPING IRON
DISLIKES: RHINOS
WEAPON: GLADIUS

SPECIAL MOVE:
SOUL STEAL — Attacks enemy while restoring some of your own health.

FIGHTING FACTS

The bestiarii were gladiators who specialized in fighting wild animals. They even had their own school where they learnt various beast-slaying techniques.

LEGENDARY

KANAR
THE ROMAN AUXILIARY

Preparing for battle as he sailed across the Gulf of Izmit, Kanar became embroiled in a dispute with a legionnaire who accused him of being a barbarian. This loyal yet volatile warrior drew his sword, but was summoned to the Wildlands before he could deliver the fatal blow.

ELEMENT: AIR
LIKES: ROMAN CULTURE
DISLIKES: LOUDMOUTHS
WEAPON: MAINZ
SPECIAL MOVE: ARMOUR BREAK —
Attacks opponent and weakens their Armour.

FIGHTING FACTS

The ultimate medal an auxiliary officer could attain was given to the first man to scale an enemy rampart. But few were awarded, as most died trying.

SUPER RARE

FLAVIA
THE ROMAN GLADIATRIX

Fearsome and feisty, Flavia decided she'd had enough of life as a gladiatrix after being forced to fight off several dwarves for the entertainment of Emperor Augustus. Thankfully, she was summoned to the Wildlands moments before the escape tunnel she had spent months digging collapsed, burying the guards pursuing her.

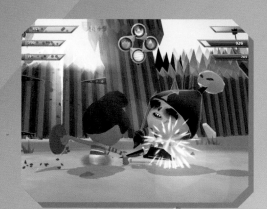

ELEMENT: EARTH
LIKES: STANDING OVATIONS
DISLIKES: DEMEANING PERFORMANCES
WEAPON: GLADIUS
SPECIAL MOVE: COUNTER BLOW —
Parry opponent's normal strikes and counter attack.

FIGHTING FACTS

Female gladiators are said to have usually fought at night, and were sometimes forced to fend off dwarves and wild animals.

SUPER RARE

WULF
THE HARII BRUTE

With his face painted a deathly shade of black, Wulf was prowling towards an enemy camp in the dead of night when suddenly the clouds cleared, bathing his shadowy army in moonlight. In the ensuing chaos this formidable warrior was whisked to the Wildlands, still clutching a freshly severed arm.

ELEMENT: EARTH
LIKES: PAINTING THINGS BLACK
DISLIKES: DAYLIGHT
WEAPON: SEAX
SPECIAL MOVE: STEALTH STRIKE — Attack enemies without tagging into the fight.

FIGHTING FACTS

Sometimes referred to as 'Ghost Warriors', the Germanic Harii terrified enemies by painting themselves black and choosing dark nights to fight.

LEGENDARY

TIBERIUS
THE ROMAN IMPERATOR

YEAR: 25 AD

Inspecting the gold mines of Las Medulas in Hispania, Tiberius was reprimanding a lazy slave when a colossal wall of water from the reservoir above came thundering through the tunnel. Swept up in the surge this fearsome leader lost consciousness, only to wake up disorientated and soggy in the Wildlands.

ELEMENT: FIRE
LIKES: GOLD NUGGETS
DISLIKES: IDLE SLAVES
WEAPON: SPATHA
SPECIAL MOVE: FIRE BOOST – Boosts FIRE damage inflicted by all team members.

FIGHTING FACTS

If a Roman emperor wanted to rid himself of a particularly bothersome senator he would simply write him a letter ordering him to kill himself.

LEGENDARY

45

RARE

LEON
THE BRAWLING GAUL

Quiet but savage, Leon helped defeat the forces of Julius Caesar in the Battle of Gergovia. Having just impaled three Roman legionaries on a single spear, this feisty warrior was attempting to skewer a centurion when he found himself summoned to the Wildlands, mid-thrust.

ELEMENT: WATER
LIKES: SPEARING ROMANS
DISLIKES: RABID DOGS
WEAPON: LONG SWORD

SPECIAL MOVE:
ICE STORM — Freeze all enemies with WATER power.

FIGHTING FACTS

During the reign of Gallic leader Vercingetorix, the last warrior to arrive at morning roll call would be tortured and killed in front of his comrades. Fair enough!

47

PACORUS
THE PARTHIAN WARRIOR

A devoted and obedient warrior, Pacorus was guarding the mint at Ecbatana when he heard the tinkling of coins. Entering the vault to investigate, he was confronted by thieves holding bulging sacks, but was summoned to the Wildlands the moment he raised his razor-sharp shamshir.

ELEMENT: EARTH
LIKES: OBEYING ORDERS
DISLIKES: SNEAKY BANDITS
WEAPON: SHAMSHIR

SPECIAL MOVE:
CLAW CRUSH — Crush enemies with the elemental power of EARTH.

FIGHTING FACTS

Armoured Parthian horsemen used long, thick lances but wielded them with such skill they could impale two men at once.

RARE

SUPER RARE

50

BOUDICA
THE ICENI WARRIOR QUEEN

Summoned as she tore through the entire Roman 9th Legion on her scythed chariot, Boudica finds life in the Wildlands frustrating because she misses leading her Iceni clan. Thankfully there are plenty of Romans around, so she cheers herself up by saving her best beatings for them.

ELEMENT: FIRE
LIKES: CHARIOT RACING
DISLIKES: BROKEN AXLES
WEAPON: LONG SWORD

SPECIAL MOVE:
SWITCH STRIKE — Target and hit a specific member of the enemy team.

FIGHTING FACTS

The Iceni would thunder through enemy forces aboard chariots fitted with huge blades on either side, ripping the Romans to bits!

SENI
THE MEROITIC WARRIOR

Having looted several gold statues from Aswan, Seni was heading home to the Kingdom of Kush when a crocodile upended his raft. Frantically swimming towards the banks of the Nile, this impetuous warrior spotted a helping hand but was zapped to the Wildlands the second he grasped it.

ELEMENT: EARTH
LIKES: THE KINGDOM OF KUSH
DISLIKES: NILE CROCODILES
WEAPON: SWORD
SPECIAL MOVE: CLAW CRUSH — Crush enemies with the elemental power of EARTH.

FIGHTING FACTS

More than two hundred pyramids mark the site of the ancient city of Meroe, once a wealthy metropolis in the Kingdom of Kush.

LEGENDARY

MAXIMUS
THE PRAETORIAN GUARD

As Emperor Nero delivered a deranged speech, Maximus spotted a blade glinting in the crowd. With lightning reactions this highly decorated guard leapt into the throng. But when the horrified masses dispersed, Maximus had vanished to the Wildlands, leaving only his dagger jammed in the would-be assassin's throat.

ELEMENT: AIR
LIKES: LOOKING FOR TROUBLE
DISLIKES: DISORDER
WEAPON: GLADIUS
SPECIAL MOVE: TORNADO STRIKE —
Blast enemies with the elemental power of AIR.

FIGHTING FACTS

Desertion in the Roman Army was punishable by 'decimation', a tradition in which a randomly chosen soldier was clubbed to death by nine comrades.

LEGENDARY

COMMON

54

BRUTUS
THE ROMAN SOLDIER

Stationed in Pompeii, Brutus was summoned to the Wildlands while attempting to control a riot triggered by an escaped tiger in the amphitheatre. This fearless soldier still misses his comrades, oblivious to the fact they perished in the cataclysmic eruption of Vesuvius the very next day.

ELEMENT: FIRE
LIKES: BAKED DORMICE
DISLIKES: BATHING
WEAPON: GLADIUS

SPECIAL MOVE:
SOUL STEAL — Attacks enemy while restoring some of your own health.

FIGHTING FACTS

The Romans used flaming pigs in battle! Coated in oil, the blazing, panic-stricken beasts would cause bacony mayhem amongst enemy horses.

CRIXUS
THE ROMAN GLADIATOR

YEAR: 112 AD

Having made his escape from the Colosseum by hiding in a cart loaded with mangled corpses, reluctant gladiator Crixus thought his fighting days were well and truly behind him. Unfortunately he was summoned to the Wildlands before he could even change out of his blood-stained loincloth.

ELEMENT: AIR
LIKES: THUMBS UP
DISLIKES: HECKLERS
WEAPON: TRIDENT

SPECIAL MOVE:
AIR BOOST – Boosts AIR damage inflicted by all team members.

FIGHTING FACTS

A gladiator's trident had a slightly longer middle spike so that opponents trapped in weighted nets could be skewered with greater ease!

RARE

VIRIATHUS
THE LUSITANIAN COMMANDER

Having just made mincemeat of the Roman-loving traitors bribed to assassinate him while he slept, Viriathus heard the clash of swords outside his burning tent. Grabbing his weapon he rushed outside, only to find himself in the Wildlands, where his glorious leadership skills now mean nothing.

ELEMENT: AIR
LIKES: PIG'S BLOOD STEW
DISLIKES: CAMPING
WEAPON: SPATHA
SPECIAL MOVE:
TORNADO STRIKE — Blast enemies with the elemental power of AIR.

FIGHTING FACTS

Heroic Lusitanian leader Viriathus is said to have slept in his armour and always kept his weapons with him.

LEGENDARY

RAVI
THE MAURYAN WARRIOR

YEAR: 263 AD

Having sworn loyalty to Ashoka the Great, Ravi sliced his way through enemies like a warrior possessed. Renowned for his ability to fell three men with a single blow, this marauding Mauryan was summoned to the Wildlands as he trampled enemy archers astride his trusty war elephant during the Kalinga War.

ELEMENT: EARTH
LIKES: THE SCENT OF BLOOD
DISLIKES: ANYONE MESSING WITH HIS ELEPHANT
WEAPON: KHANDA SWORD
SPECIAL MOVE:
SWITCH STRIKE — Target and hit a specific member of the enemy team.

FIGHTING FACTS

Indian war elephants had long daggers attached to their tusks, and were trained to execute prisoners by stomping on their heads.

SUPER RARE

ANIL
THE GUPTA WARRIOR

Attempting to subdue a local uprising in the Himalayas, Anil was forced by angry villagers to retreat into a cave. Surrounded but reluctant to surrender, this wild warrior decided to bow out in a blaze of glory, but when he emerged from the darkness he was alone in the Wildlands.

ELEMENT: FIRE
LIKES: MOUSTACHE GROOMING
DISLIKES: LOCAL POLITICS
WEAPON: KHANDA
SPECIAL MOVE: INFERNO – Burn enemies with the elemental power of FIRE.

FIGHTING FACTS

Warriors of the Gupta Empire used iron shafts to repel war elephants, flaming arrows in sieges and battles, and sophisticated war machines to enter cities.

LEGENDARY

GOAR
THE ALANS WARRIOR

Having crossed the Pyrenees with a bunch of Alans, Goar was strutting through Lusitania looking for trouble when he stumbled across a scene of carnage. Rummaging through a pile of corpses, this heartless warrior spotted a glowing blue gem but was summoned to the Wildlands the second he grasped it.

ELEMENT: AIR
LIKES: LOOTING
DISLIKES: TAINTED TREASURE
WEAPON: SEAX
SPECIAL MOVE: TORNADO STRIKE —
Blast enemies with the elemental power of AIR.

FIGHTING FACTS

When the Alans settled in Lusitania they are thought to have introduced to Europe the Alaunt, a massive hunting and fighting dog which is now extinct.

COMMON

GUNTHER
THE BRUTAL BURGUNDIAN

Summoned to the Wildlands while knee-deep in Rhineland mud, Gunther loves reminiscing about the days when he would defeat several Hun mercenaries before breakfast. Unfortunately, few of his fellow warriors bother listening because this battle-hardened fighter can't help making mincemeat of onlookers whenever he re-enacts his greatest slayings.

ELEMENT: WATER
LIKES: OUTRIGHT VICTORY
DISLIKES: SHAVING
WEAPON: AXE

SPECIAL MOVE:
ARMOUR BREAK —
Attack opponent and
weaken their Armour.

FIGHTING FACTS

Burgundian king Gundahar is said to have plotted with a Roman general to get rid of Emperor Athemius, but eventually beheaded him himself!

RARE

HUNERIC
THE VANDAL KING

?

Summoned as he prepared to smash a jagged rock over the head of yet another pretender to his throne, Huneric wanders the Wildlands searching for his beloved wife. Unfortunately, his failure to find her has made him even more ferocious than he was back in his regal heyday.

ELEMENT: FIRE
LIKES: AIMLESS WANDERING
DISLIKES: CIVILITY
WEAPON: LONG SEAX
SPECIAL MOVE: SURPRISE –
Performs a randomly selected Special Move.

FIGHTING FACTS

When the Vandals sacked Rome in 455 AD they destroyed many objects of cultural significance, hence the term 'vandalism'.

LEGENDARY

RARE

BOTHERIC
THE RECKLESS OSTROGOTH

Brave but bloodthirsty, Botheric was summoned to the Wildlands just after he had bumped off the King of Italy and all his men during a peace banquet in Ravenna. Nowadays this sullen warrior goes from battle to battle forever wondering what was for dessert.

ELEMENT: AIR
LIKES: WILD FEASTS
DISLIKES: LAUGHTER
WEAPON: LONG SEAX

SPECIAL MOVE:
STEALTH ASSAULT —
Attack all enemies without tagging into the fight.

FIGHTING FACTS

Having invited the King of Italy to a feast, Ostrogoth leader Theoderic the Great killed him and had his family wiped out.

BALASH
THE SASSANID WARRIOR

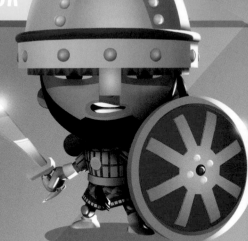

Scaling the walls of the fortress city of Amida alongside the King of Persia, Balash was dodging rocks hurled by Romans when a direct hit slammed his helmet down over his eyes. Readjusting it with his shield, this intrepid warrior looked up to find himself alone in the Wildlands.

ELEMENT: AIR
LIKES: SIEGE WARFARE
DISLIKES: ILL-FITTING HELMETS
WEAPON: LONG SWORD
SPECIAL MOVE: TEMPEST –
Blast all enemies with AIR power.

FIGHTING FACTS

Sassanid archers would shower the enemy with storms of arrows, and if forced to retreat would even fire backwards as they fled!

SUPER RARE

COMMON

OSGOOD
THE SAXON DESTROYER

Thanks to his exploits battling the forces of King Arthur, Osgood was already a living legend when he eviscerated a dozen traitors in Britannia. But even this cold-blooded warrior could not avoid being summoned to the Wildlands, because it happened while he was sleeping off a hornful of potent mead.

ELEMENT: EARTH
LIKES: PUNISHING WEAKNESS
DISLIKES: BURNING CAKES
WEAPON: LONG SWORD
SPECIAL MOVE: BOULDER BASH – Crush all enemies with EARTH power.

FIGHTING FACTS

As well as battleaxes and daggers, most Saxons carried thrusting spears that they used to jab the face, eyes and upper body of an opponent. In your face!

YEAR: 602 AD

SIMO
THE GOKTURK GENERAL

Stripped of his royal title due to a military mishap, Simo was tormenting troops beneath the Great Wall of China when an earthquake struck. Ordering his men to flee, this noble warrior tried to sidestep falling masonry but tumbled into a rapidly expanding crack and found himself in the Wildlands.

ELEMENT: WATER
LIKES: ROYAL LIVING
DISLIKES: DEMOTION
WEAPON: KILIJ SWORD
SPECIAL MOVE: WATER BOOST – Boosts WATER damage inflicted by all team members.

FIGHTING FACTS

Bumin, founder of the Gokturk Empire, overthrew the Rouran leader Anagui and killed his emissary after he accused him of being his 'slave and blacksmith'. Touchy!

SUPER RARE

ERIKA
THE VIKING SHIELD MAIDEN

With her fiery temper, it's no surprise Erika was summoned to the Wildlands while wreaking blood-spattered mayhem. But she was wreaking it against her Viking shipmates after they mocked her for showing a kidnapped priest mercy, gutting the lot of them before they had even finished laughing!

ELEMENT: AIR
LIKES: INVADING FOREIGN LANDS
DISLIKES: BEING LAUGHED AT
WEAPON: LONG SWORD
SPECIAL MOVE: TEMPEST —
Blast all enemies with AIR power.

FIGHTING FACTS

Viking axes were capable of cutting through iron helmets and splicing down through the skull, coming to rest near the teeth! Now that's gotta hurt!

SUPER RARE

71

YEAR: 623 AD

PING
THE TANG DYNASTY PRINCESS

Guest of honour at an imperial banquet in Chang'an, Ping was hoping to be lauded for her victories on the battlefield. Instead, she was nearly assassinated by an infatuated servant armed with a sharpened chopstick. Deflecting the blow, she tumbled beneath the table only to find herself in the Wildlands.

ELEMENT: AIR
LIKES: REARING SILK WORMS
DISLIKES: LOVESICK SERVANTS
WEAPON: JIAN

SPECIAL MOVE:
TEMPEST – Blast all enemies with AIR power.

FIGHTING FACTS

In ancient China, treason was often punishable via 'Death by a Thousand Cuts', a technique that involved slicing off portions of flesh over an extended period.

LEGENDARY

BRETH
THE PICT WARRIOR

Summoned to the Wildlands while slaying Northumbrians during the Battle of Dun Nechtain, Breth is feared for his unbridled aggression and violent temper. Perhaps that is because his only son was captured by enemy forces on the shores of Loch Insh just before the fighting broke out.

ELEMENT: WATER
LIKES: FISHING
DISLIKES: NORTHUMBRIANS
WEAPON: LONG SWORD
SPECIAL MOVE: PHANTOM SHIELD –
Boosts the Armour strength of all team members.

FIGHTING FACTS

The Picts favoured two forms of execution: drowning and beheading, both of which were pretty tame considering the era.

SUPER RARE

AGE OF EMPIRE

4. GUNNAR

2. ARDO

5. MALIK

1. KWAN THE HWARANG WARRIOR
689 AD, SILLA

2. ARDO THE VICIOUS VISIGOTH
711 AD, VISIGOTHIC EMPIRE

3. MOHINDER THE RAJPUT WARRIOR
738 AD, RAJASTHAN

4. GUNNAR THE VIKING RAIDER
798 AD, MEDIEVAL SCANDINAVIA

5. MALIK THE UMAYYAD WARRIOR
920 AD, EMIRATE OF CORDOVA

6. ZAFIR THE FATIMID WARRIOR
969 AD, EGYPT

7. YING THE SONG DYNASTY WARRIOR
971 AD, SONG DYNASTY CHINA

8. GRIM THE VARANGIAN MERCENARY
988 AD, BYZANTINE EMPIRE

9. VOLTEN THE BYZANTINE WARRIOR
1071 AD, BYZANTINE EMPIRE

10. ANCHALY THE KHMER WARRIOR
1114 AD, KHMER EMPIRE

9. VOLTEN

8. GRIM

7. YING

6. ZAFIR

1. KWAN

10. ANCHALY

3. MOHINDER

N
W E
S

KWAN
THE HWARANG WARRIOR

Kwan loves brawling even more than he loves himself, but as a Hwarang warrior that is to be expected. More surprising is the fact he was once a revered general in 7th century Silla, and was summoned to the Wildlands after receiving an electric shock while flying a communication kite.

ELEMENT: WATER
LIKES: BEHEADING FLOWERS
DISLIKES: KITES
WEAPON: GEOM
SPECIAL MOVE: WATER BOOST – Temporarily increase WATER damage inflicted by all team members.

FIGHTING FACTS

Despite their tough image, the elite Hwarang (or 'Flower Boys') of Silla were originally known for their flamboyant use of make-up and accessories.

SUPER RARE

ARDO
THE VICIOUS VISIGOTH

Battling invading Umayyad forces in Hispania, Ardo lost his weapon and was forced to smash his attackers in the face with his iron helmet. But, having finished off every enemy in sight, this barbarous warrior was unceremoniously summoned to the Wildlands while relieving himself against an olive tree.

ELEMENT: WATER
LIKES: BRUTAL BATTLE
DISLIKES: FIDDLY ARMOUR
WEAPON: LONG SEAX
SPECIAL MOVE: TEAM STRIKE — Draws health from entire team to strike enemies.

FIGHTING FACTS

It is said that King Roderic of the Visigoths arrived at the Battle of Guadalete in a chariot drawn by eight white mules!

RARE

MOHINDER
THE RAJPUT WARRIOR

Summoned as the Battle of Rajasthan reached its grisly climax, Mohinder was causing carnage with his razor-sharp khanda when he saw an enemy camel stumbling towards him. Dodging the mortally wounded beast, this tenacious warrior felt himself being enveloped in energy before coming round in the Wildlands, bloodied and bewildered.

ELEMENT: FIRE
LIKES: THE SMELL OF VICTORY
DISLIKES: THE UNFAMILIAR STENCH OF DEFEAT
WEAPON: KHANDA
SPECIAL MOVE: FIRE BOOST – Boosts FIRE damage inflicted by all team members.

FIGHTING FACTS

Rajput warriors hated losing, so much so they would throw themselves into certain death on the battlefield to avoid the shame of surrender.

SUPER RARE

TOKI
THE VIKING WARRIOR

Famed for his heroism and swordsmanship, Toki was summoned to the Wildlands as he leapt from his blazing longship during a calamitous dawn raid. But all that seems like a distant memory now, and if it weren't for the scorch marks on his shield, Toki would be certain he dreamt it.

ELEMENT: AIR
LIKES: THINKING OF HOME
DISLIKES: INJUSTICE
WEAPON: LONG SWORD

SPECIAL MOVE:
TORNADO STRIKE — Blast enemies with the elemental power of AIR.

FIGHTING FACTS

Vikings settled arguments via 'ordeals', painful tests of bravery that included picking stones out of boiling water and carrying hunks of red-hot iron.

COMMON

GUNNAR
THE VIKING RAIDER

Summoned to the Wildlands shortly after looting three monasteries in two days, Gunnar is convinced he is now living in Valhalla. He loves recounting the tale of how he once freed his longboat from a frozen fjord by praying to Thor and smashing the ice with his bare hands.

ELEMENT: EARTH
LIKES: RAIDING AND TRADING
DISLIKES: CLERGYMEN
WEAPON: LONG SWORD

SPECIAL MOVE: BERSERK — Drains some health and attacks opponents.

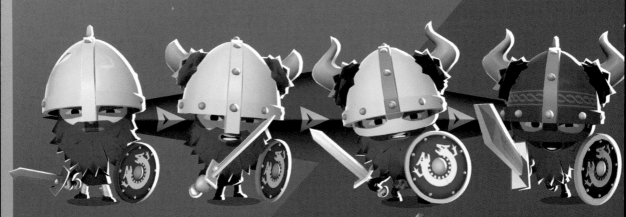

FIGHTING FACTS

Contrary to popular belief, there is no significant evidence that Vikings ever wore horned helmets. But try telling Gunnar that!

COMMON

RARE

MALIK
THE UMAYYAD WARRIOR

Celebrated throughout Al-Andalus for his bravery, Malik found himself in the Wildlands after running through a mysterious doorway in a bustling bazaar while pursuing a Frankish assassin. With his gleaming scimitar and mind-blowing regenerative powers, Malik remains a most relentless warrior!

ELEMENT: WATER
LIKES: DUELLING
DISLIKES: SAND FLIES
WEAPON: SCIMITAR

SPECIAL MOVE:
REGENERATION – Gradually restores health to all team members.

FIGHTING FACTS

Umayyad fighters loved their scimitars because they could pull them through flesh without fear of the curved blade sticking. Perfect for slashing bodies to bits!

BORIS
THE KIEVAN KNIGHT

Rumoured to be the brother of Vladimir the Great, Boris was drinking wine in the Khazar fortress of Sarkel when he tripped over a severed leg, fell in the Don River and came round in the Wildlands. Now convinced he's immortal, this surly knight claims to be impervious to pain.

ELEMENT: FIRE
LIKES: WINE
DISLIKES: MERCY
WEAPON: ARMING SWORD

SPECIAL MOVE:
FIRE STORM — Burn all enemies with FIRE power.

FIGHTING FACTS

When the Drevlians sent twenty of their best men to persuade Princess Olga of Kiev to marry their prince, she had them buried alive. Romantic!

RARE

RARE

86

ZAFIR
THE FATIMID WARRIOR

Stationed in Cairo following the Fatimid invasion of Egypt, Zafir was admiring the majesty of the pyramids at sunrise when he felt himself being dragged into the sand. Struggling against an unseen force, this proud warrior was swallowed by the desert and transported to the Wildlands before he could scream.

ELEMENT:	EARTH	**SPECIAL MOVE:**	
LIKES:	CAMEL RACING	ROLLING THUNDER —	
DISLIKES:	SAND	Strikes three random	
WEAPON:	SCIMITAR	opponents.	

FIGHTING FACTS

The scimitar's curved blade was designed for slicing at enemies from horseback, and could sever limbs in one stroke.

YING
THE SONG DYNASTY WARRIOR

Battling the mighty war elephant corps of the Southern Han army, Ying was reloading his crossbow when he remembered it was his youngest son's birthday. Temporarily distracted, this culture-loving warrior closed his eyes and began humming a lullaby. When he opened them again, he was alone in the Wildlands.

ELEMENT: FIRE
LIKES: LANTERN FESTIVALS
DISLIKES: CROSSBOW BLISTERS
WEAPON: DAO WAR SWORD

SPECIAL MOVE:
COUNTER BLOW —
Parry opponent's normal strikes and counter attack.

FIGHTING FACTS

As well as crossbows, Song warriors are known to have used double-piston pump flamethrowers to roast attackers!

RARE

89

RARE

IVAN
THE RUS BOGATYR

After vowing not to shave until he had bumped off at least fifty Tatar invaders, Ivan spotted a group of weedy-looking raiders and was looking forward to a smooth chin. But just as he raised his sword, this rowdy warrior was summoned to the Wildlands, beard and all!

ELEMENT:	FIRE	**SPECIAL MOVE:**
LIKES:	THE BUZZ OF BATTLE	PHANTOM STRIKE –
DISLIKES:	STUBBLE	Inflicts high physical
WEAPON:	SWORD	damage on all enemies.

FIGHTING FACTS

When Vladimir the Great died, his body was dismembered so that the various bits could be worshipped as relics in different places.

GRIM
THE VARANGIAN MERCENARY

Brave but disloyal, Grim chose to betray Basil II in exchange for a barrel of potent ale. But this devious warrior's bad luck was the Emperor's good fortune when he was summoned to the Wildlands from a souk in Constantinople while planning murder most foul with his fellow mercenaries.

ELEMENT: AIR
LIKES: BRIBERY AND CORRUPTION
DISLIKES: OATHS
WEAPON: LONG SWORD
SPECIAL MOVE: TEMPEST – Blast all enemies with AIR power.

FIGHTING FACTS

Members of the Varangian Guard used fearsome long axes capable of splitting a torso in two, or hacking off a horse's head with a single blow!

SUPER RARE

YEAR: 1066 AD

EVERARD
THE NORMAN WARRIOR

As the Battle of Hastings raged around him, Everard spotted King Harold himself issuing orders atop a hillock. Drawing back his bow, this ruthless Norman warrior fired straight at the king's eye but was promptly knocked unconscious by a flying severed head. He woke up befuddled in the Wildlands.

ELEMENT: FIRE
LIKES: TARGET PRACTICE
DISLIKES: ENGLISH WEATHER
WEAPON: ARMING SWORD

SPECIAL MOVE:
HEALING — Restores health to your most wounded team mate.

FIGHTING FACTS

William the Conqueror's body exploded as priests attempted to stuff it in its coffin. Apparently they pushed on the bloated abdomen, causing it to burst. Yuck!

RARE

94

VOLTEN
THE BYZANTINE WARRIOR

Ruthless and disloyal, Volten deserted the Byzantine army during the chaotic Battle of Manzikert. He was hoping to swap sides and join forces with the Turko-Persian enemy, but found himself summoned to the Wildlands while attempting to steal a fallen warrior's uniform.

ELEMENT: FIRE
LIKES: GOLD COINS
DISLIKES: BLIND LOYALTY
WEAPON: SPATHION
SPECIAL MOVE: INFERNO —
Burn enemies with the elemental power of FIRE.

FIGHTING FACTS

Byzantine warriors used primitive flamethrowers to spew flaming liquid at enemy ships and attacking forces. Highly effective, the mysterious concoction could even burn on water.

SUPER RARE

95

YEAR: 1099 AD

RODRIGO
THE CASTILIAN WARRIOR

A revered nobleman, Rodrigo was defending Valencia from marauding Berbers when his horse began to act strangely. Dismounting, he noticed a golden talisman glinting in the beast's fresh manure. Upon picking it up, this military genius was summoned to the Wildlands before he could even wipe his gauntlets!

ELEMENT: EARTH
LIKES: BRAINSTORMING SESSIONS
DISLIKES: TWITCHY HORSES
WEAPON: TIZONA
SPECIAL MOVE: BOMBARD — Calls a delayed air strike on whichever opponent is on screen.

FIGHTING FACTS

El Cid's wife is said to have had his corpse fitted with armour and set atop his horse to boost the morale of his troops.

LEGENDARY

ANCHALY
THE KHMER WARRIOR

YEAR: 1114 AD

On night duty guarding the newly constructed temple of Angkor Wat, this impulsive warrior spotted an imposing figure lurking behind a palm tree. Deciding to attack, Anchaly raised his weapon but was instantly summoned to the Wildlands, blissfully unaware of the fact he had almost decapitated King Suryavarman II.

ELEMENT: FIRE
LIKES: BEING SPONTANEOUS
DISLIKES: RETICULATED PYTHONS
WEAPON: DHA
SPECIAL MOVE: ROLLING THUNDER — Strikes three random opponents.

FIGHTING FACTS

Angkorian ruler Suryavarman II often went into battle leading over a thousand elephants formed into squadrons protected by infantry and cavalry.

LEGENDARY

AGE OF HONOUR

3. WALLACE

5. SOARING EAGLE

7. FURIO

10. KOFI

1. **LANCE** THE KNIGHT TEMPLAR
   1177 AD, MEDIEVAL ENGLAND

2. **KHUTULUN** THE MONGOL PRINCESS
   1300 AD, MEDIEVAL MONGOLIA

3. **WALLACE** THE SCOTTISH HIGHLANDER
   1297 AD, MEDIEVAL SCOTLAND

4. **WU** THE SHAOLIN MONK
   1379 AD, NORTHERN WEI DYNASTY CHINA

5. **SOARING EAGLE** THE APACHE SCOUT
   1391 AD, FIRST NATION AMERICAS

6. **SAKUMA** THE LONE SAMURAI
   1397 AD, FEUDAL JAPAN

7. **FURIO** THE FLORENTINE KNIGHT
   1399 AD, MEDIEVAL REPUBLIC OF FLORENCE

8. **DOONGARA** THE AUSTRALIAN ABORIGINE
   1400 AD, PITJANTJATJARA

9. **JOAN** THE WARRIOR MAID
   1431 AD, ORLEANS MEDIEVAL FRANCE

10. **KOFI** THE BENIN BODYGUARD
    1468 AD, BENIN EMPIRE

1. LANCE

2. KHUTULUN

6. SAKUMA

9. JOAN

4. WU

8. DOONGARA

N
W · E
S

LEROC
THE KNIGHT HOSPITALLER

The last thing LeRoc remembers before waking up in the Wildlands is plummeting from a crumbling tower shortly after it was struck by lightning during the Siege of Ascalon. Perhaps that explains why this noble knight can now summon deadly lightning bolts during battle.

ELEMENT: AIR
LIKES: SIEGES
DISLIKES: RUSTY GAUNTLETS
WEAPON: MACE

SPECIAL MOVE:
THUNDER STRIKE —
Electrocute enemies with the power of lightning.

FIGHTING FACTS

Several leading Hospitallers lost their heads during the Siege of Ascalon. Literally, because they were chopped off and sent to the caliph in Cairo!

COMMON

RARE

LANCE
THE KNIGHT TEMPLAR

YEAR:
1177 AD

Laying waste to Saladin's dwindling troops during the epic Battle of Montgisard, Lance was momentarily distracted by the sight of the Sultan fleeing the carnage on a racing camel. Just as this chivalrous knight had commandeered a steed to join the pursuit, he was summoned to the Wildlands.

ELEMENT: EARTH
LIKES: SPREADING THE WORD
DISLIKES: ITCHY CHAINMAIL
WEAPON: ARMING SWORD

SPECIAL MOVE:
THUNDER STRIKE —
Electrocute enemies with the power of lightning.

FIGHTING FACTS

During the Battle of Montgisard the teenage king, Baldwin IV, fought with bandaged hands to protect his leprosy-ravaged flesh.

YEAR:
1180 AD

BENKEI
THE SOHEI WARRIOR MONK

Crossing the Uji River, Benkei was using his lightning reactions to dodge enemy arrows when he saw Prince Mochihito tussling with several Taira warriors. Turning to help, this silent but violent monk slipped on fallen cherry blossom, somersaulted in the air and landed in the Wildlands with a bump.

ELEMENT: WATER
LIKES: CHANTING
DISLIKES: SQUISHED CHERRY BLOSSOM
WEAPON: KATANA
SPECIAL MOVE: STEALTH ASSAULT – Attack all enemies without tagging into the fight.

FIGHTING FACTS

Although warrior monks were accomplished archers they also used the kanabo, a solid iron club that was mostly used to defeat opponents without bloodshed.

LEGENDARY

KAZUMI
THE SAMURAI BRIDE

YEAR:
1184 AD

Legendary samurai Kazumi
was summoned to the
Wildlands as the Battle of
Awazu raged around her.
Having decapitated several
enemies, she was taking cover behind
a fallen horse when she felt a strange
sensation. Now, desperate to re-engage the enemy,
she lashes out at everyone she encounters.

ELEMENT: WATER
LIKES: ARCHERY
DISLIKES: EELS
WEAPON: NAGINATA
SPECIAL MOVE: STEALTH STRIKE –
Attack all enemies without tagging into the fight.

FIGHTING FACTS

At up to 8ft long, the naginata gave
female samurai a big reach advantage,
and was ideal for planting in the
ground to rip apart oncoming horses.

SUPER RARE

105

RARE

OTTO
THE TEUTONIC KNIGHT

Feared for his ruthless efficiency, Otto has not spoken a word in years. Maybe that's because he is still in shock, having been summoned to the Wildlands seconds before a bunch of Prussian pagans were about to make his tongue into a belt.

ELEMENT: AIR
LIKES: CONVERTING PAGANS
DISLIKES: SMALL TALK
WEAPON: MACE
SPECIAL MOVE: SOUL STEAL — Attacks enemy while restoring some of your own health.

FIGHTING FACTS

During 1242's Battle of the Ice, Teutonic Knights retreated across frozen Lake Peipus, but their heavy armour caused the ice to break and many drowned.

107

ZENGIS
THE MONGOL WARRIOR

Zengis still refuses to admit that he found himself in the Wildlands after being thrown from his horse on a mountain pass. But that's hardly surprising, because this sabre-wielding warrior is legendary for leading brutal campaigns on horseback against the Jin Dynasty. Don't make him angry!

ELEMENT:	WATER	**SPECIAL MOVE:**
LIKES:	HIS HORSE	FROZEN CRUNCH — Freeze and
DISLIKES:	DESERTERS	shatter your enemies with the
WEAPON:	SABRE	elemental power of WATER.

FIGHTING FACTS

Mongol soldiers sometimes mounted attacks using helpless African prisoners as body shields.

COMMON

DAO
THE TRAN DYNASTY WARRIOR

Retreating from Mongol invaders led by the mighty Kublai Khan, Dao was obeying 'scorched earth' orders to destroy villages and crops when he spotted an abandoned boat drifting along the Red River. Fascinated, he attempted to leap aboard but was summoned to the Wildlands before hitting the deck.

ELEMENT: FIRE
LIKES: POMP AND CEREMONY
DISLIKES: GIANT LEECHES
WEAPON: DHA
SPECIAL MOVE: TEAM STRIKE — Draws health from entire team to strike enemies.

FIGHTING FACTS

Tran warriors defeated invading Chinese forces by driving iron-tipped stakes into the bed of the Bach Dang River, trapping and impaling the entire Mongol fleet.

LEGENDARY

WALLACE
THE SCOTTISH HIGHLANDER

Charging at retreating English forces with frenzied abandon, Wallace was halfway across Stirling Bridge when it collapsed. Tumbling into the River Forth, this heroic Highlander felt countless bodies raining down on him, but when the pandemonium subsided he found himself in the Wildlands — cold, wet and confused.

ELEMENT: WATER
LIKES: BLOODY MAYHEM
DISLIKES: THE ENGLISH
WEAPON: CLAYMORE
SPECIAL MOVE: BOMBARD —
Calls a delayed air strike on whichever opponent is on screen.

FIGHTING FACTS

Scottish rebel William Wallace had the English treasurer Hugh de Cressingham flayed before making a sword belt from a strip of his skin.

LEGENDARY

KHUTULUN
THE MONGOL PRINCESS

Riding into an enemy camp, Khutulun was attempting to rescue several captives when she spotted her cousin Kublai Khan strutting around issuing orders. But as she dismounted to investigate, this heroic warrior princess trod on a sleeping dog and was summoned to the Wildlands the second it started yelping.

ELEMENT: EARTH
LIKES: WRESTLING
DISLIKES: YAPPY DOGS
WEAPON: SABRE
SPECIAL MOVE: BOULDER BASH — Crush all enemies with EARTH power.

FIGHTING FACTS

Mongol princess Khutulun insisted that any man wishing to marry her must wrestle her and forfeit their horses if they lost. She gained 10,000 horses defeating prospective suitors!

LEGENDARY

ABU
THE MAMLUK WARRIOR SLAVE

Having repelled both the Mongols and the Crusaders, Abu was settling down to life as the sultan's chief assassin. But his days as a covert cut-throat were numbered because he was summoned to the Wildlands just as he was about to behead his fifth target, a treacherous viceroy.

ELEMENT: FIRE
LIKES: CUTTING AND THRUSTING
DISLIKES: CARRIER PIGEONS
WEAPON: SCIMITAR

SPECIAL MOVE: INFERNO — Burn your enemies with the elemental power of FIRE.

FIGHTING FACTS

Mamluks were slave warriors who rose to become rulers of Egypt and Syria. Mamluk-based regimes thrived in Ottoman provinces as late as the 19th century.

COMMON

HUA
THE MING SPY

A loyal spy for the Hongwu Emperor, Hua was posing as an entertainer at a Mongol banquet when a nosy juggler blew her cover. Fending off guards with just a small fruit knife, she leapt from the balcony on to a canopy, which catapulted her straight into the Wildlands.

ELEMENT: FIRE
LIKES: PRICELESS VASES
DISLIKES: CROUCHING TIGERS
WEAPON: DAO
SPECIAL MOVE: STEALTH STRIKE — Attack enemies without tagging into the fight.

FIGHTING FACTS

Emperor Zhengde sometimes decorated his palace to resemble a town and forced staff to dress like peasants so he could stroll around like a normal person.

SUPER RARE

WU
THE SHAOLIN MONK

Before being summoned to the Wildlands, Wu commanded a ruthless mercenary strike force from a mountain top monastery in central China. Renowned for his stealth, this merciless monk possesses mystical healing powers and frequently meditates before making monastic mincemeat of opponents.

ELEMENT: AIR
LIKES: SILENCE
DISLIKES: JAPANESE PIRATES
WEAPON: JIAN
SPECIAL MOVE: REGENERATION — Gradually restores health to all team members.

FIGHTING FACTS

The 'Diamond Finger' is a Shaolin move designed to mangle opponents' internal organs by tapping on the chest. It can take over three years to master.

LEGENDARY

COMMON

BLAINE
THE GAELIC KERN

Swift and ferocious, Blaine misses the days when he would gallop away from cattle raids with a few severed heads dangling from his horse. In fact it was during just such a raid that he was summoned to the Wildlands while under intense javelin fire.

ELEMENT:	EARTH	**SPECIAL MOVE:**
LIKES:	DEAFENING WAR CRIES	REGENERATION —
DISLIKES:	WEARING ARMOUR	Gradually restores health
WEAPON:	SPARTH AXE	to all team members.

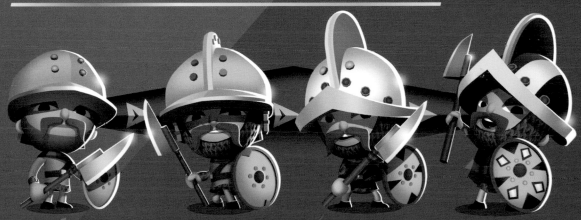

FIGHTING FACTS

Unlike wood axes, sparth axes were designed to chop through legs and arms and cause deep wounds, so vicious narrow blades were the norm.

SOARING EAGLE
THE APACHE SCOUT

Summoned to the Wildlands during a late night buffalo raid, Soaring Eagle is renowned for his ability to concoct powerful, energy-sapping poisons. When he's not extracting lethal venom or hurling his axe in fury, this brave nomad gazes at the night sky, dreaming of home.

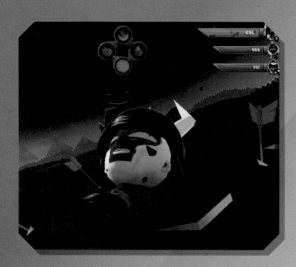

ELEMENT: EARTH
LIKES: HUNTING PRONGHORNS
DISLIKES: RAIN DANCES
WEAPON: TOMAHAWK AXE
SPECIAL MOVE: POISON —
Drain enemies slowly with Poison.

FIGHTING FACTS

Contrary to popular belief, victims did not have to be dead to be scalped by an Apache. Bad hair day? You bet!

SUPER RARE

119

COMMON

SAKUMA
THE LONE SAMURAI

Banished from his clan for breaking the samurai code, disobeying orders and slicing off his master's head, Sakuma was summoned to the Wildlands while single-handedly defending the ancient city of Kitsuki with just his wits, his katana and a broken chigiriki.

ELEMENT: AIR
LIKES: SAKE
DISLIKES: BLUNT BLADES
WEAPON: KATANA

SPECIAL MOVE:
PHANTOM STRIKE –
Inflicts high physical
damage to all enemies.

FIGHTING FACTS

Despite being taught flower arranging, samurai warriors would often test a newly forged katana's sharpness by beheading hapless peasants.

121

YEAR:
1399 AD

FURIO
THE FLORENTINE KNIGHT

Furio was a ferocious warrior but away from the battlefield he enjoyed wine, women and song — a lifestyle that finally caught up with him when he was sentenced to death for accidentally disembowelling an enraged husband. Thankfully Furio was summoned to the Wildlands just before the axe fell.

ELEMENT: AIR
LIKES: MERRIMENT
DISLIKES: JEALOUS HUSBANDS
WEAPON: ITALIAN SWORD
SPECIAL MOVE: TEAM STRIKE — Draws health from entire team to strike enemies.

FIGHTING FACTS

In medieval Italy, military disobedience was often punished by hanging offenders upside down, legs apart, and sawing them in half. Ouch!

SUPER RARE

DOONGARA
THE AUSTRALIAN ABORIGINE

Returning home from a coming-of-age ceremony beneath Uluru, Doongara was bitten by a scorpion lurking in his didgeridoo. Delirious, he staggered into the vast Outback where he spotted an amulet glinting in the sand. Upon picking it up he was whisked to the Wildlands, healed and infused with indescribable power.

ELEMENT: EARTH
LIKES: CAVE PAINTING
DISLIKES: ARACHNIDS
WEAPON: MULGA WOOD CLUB
SPECIAL MOVE: CLAW CRUSH —
Crush the enemy with EARTH power.

FIGHTING FACTS

In experienced hands the boomerang was a deadly weapon, capable of killing both kangaroos and enemy warriors. Some even featured sharpened ends for disembowelling!

LEGENDARY

JOAN
THE WARRIOR MAID

Captured while attacking Burgundians in the Ardennes, Joan was sentenced to death by burning at the stake. Thankfully, unbeknown to her executioners, she was summoned to the Wildlands just as the flames were about to engulf her. She now spends her non-fighting moments trying to discover why she was saved.

ELEMENT: WATER
LIKES: BUCKETS OF WATER
DISLIKES: THE ENGLISH
WEAPON: ÉPÉE BATARDE
SPECIAL MOVE: ICE STORM —
Freeze all enemies with WATER power.

FIGHTING FACTS

Joan of Arc inspired the 'bob' haircut. Apparently the voices that commanded the teenage Joan to don men's clothing also told her to crop her long hair.

LEGENDARY

KASIM
THE OTTOMAN WARRIOR

Bewildered by a lunar eclipse during the Fall of Constantinople, Kasim became separated from his comrades and found himself in a fierce tussle with Emperor Constantine himself! Drawing back to deliver the final blow, this fierce Ottoman warrior tumbled into a cellar and came round in the Wildlands.

ELEMENT: WATER
LIKES: TOTAL ANNIHILATION
DISLIKES: GHERKINS
WEAPON: SCIMITAR
SPECIAL MOVE: FROZEN CRUNCH — Freeze and shatter your enemies with the elemental power of WATER.

FIGHTING FACTS

Newly appointed Ottoman sultans would execute all of their brothers in order to reduce the number of claimants to the throne. Harsh!

SUPER RARE

YEAR: 1456 AD

IRONHART
THE LANCASTRIAN KNIGHT

Strutting across a corpse-strewn drawbridge, IronHart was attacking an enemy castle when he stepped aside to avoid a downpour of molten lead. Tumbling into a bloody moat, this gallant knight was fighting against the weight of his armour but finally managed to surface, only to find himself in the Wildlands!

ELEMENT: EARTH
LIKES: THE SMELL OF COLD METAL
DISLIKES: A LACK OF CHIVALRY
WEAPON: ARMING SWORD
SPECIAL MOVE: BOULDER BASH —
Crush all enemies with EARTH power.

FIGHTING FACTS

English Knights often used lethal spiked maces called 'holy water sprinklers' to penetrate plate-armour, rip flesh apart and smash skulls to smithereens. Amen!

SUPER RARE

CUTBERT
THE YORKIST KNIGHT

Trudging from a snowy battlefield following an early victory during the War of the Roses, Cutbert was wondering if his weapon was blunt when he was surrounded by enraged Lancastrians. Heroic as ever, this formidable knight attacked but was summoned to the Wildlands just as he raised his axe.

ELEMENT: WATER
LIKES: WHITE ROSES
DISLIKES: RED ROSES
WEAPON: AXE
SPECIAL MOVE:
ICE STORM — Freeze all enemies with WATER power.

FIGHTING FACTS

Treacherous Yorkist George Plantagenet is said to have been executed by being drowned in a barrel of Malmsey wine.

SUPER RARE

KOFI
THE BENIN BODYGUARD

Summoned to the Wildlands halfway through an almighty rumble in the jungle, former royal guard Kofi is a loyal but cunning warrior who can crush opponents in just a few moves. Expect no mercy from this fearless fighter — he is at his most dangerous when threatened!

ELEMENT: WATER
LIKES: SNAKES
DISLIKES: SUPERNATURAL RITUALS
WEAPON: ADA
SPECIAL MOVE: POISON HIVE —
Drain all enemies slowly with poison.

FIGHTING FACTS

Benin Warriors wore bells called egogos to warn the enemy they were on their way.

LEGENDARY

JIN
THE MING WARRIOR

Jin spent many years battling barbarians during the peak of the Ming Dynasty. Summoned to the Wildlands just before a royal audience in the Forbidden City, this battle-hardened veteran remains a ruthless fighter. But he is yet to find out what the Emperor wanted.

ELEMENT: EARTH
LIKES: BASHING BARBARIANS
DISLIKES: BETRAYAL
WEAPON: JIAN
SPECIAL MOVE:
PHANTOM STRIKE – Inflicts high physical damage to all enemies.

FIGHTING FACTS

Known as the 'Gentleman of Weapons', jian swords were double-edged and often featured sharp metal tassels to flay opponents when swept across the face.

RARE

RARE

130

AKA
THE ZANDE WARRIOR

Aka became convinced he was destined for greatness following a vision in which he saw himself battling gleaming monsters with metal skin. But having arrived in the Wildlands after a near-death experience in the raging Dungu River, Aka now knows these monsters are commonplace. And they carry swords!

ELEMENT: EARTH
LIKES: SHARPENING HIS TEETH
DISLIKES: VOICES IN HIS HEAD
WEAPON: MAKRAKA SWORD

SPECIAL MOVE:
CLAW CRUSH —
Crush the enemy
with EARTH power.

FIGHTING FACTS

As if brandishing a fierce scythe-like weapon was not enough, many Zande warriors sharpened their teeth to intimidate the enemy.

VLAD
THE WALLACHIAN COUNT

Having just impaled his sixteenth victim of the day, Vlad was striding towards the banks of the Danube when he spotted a bat fluttering into a cave. Eager to skewer something different, he dashed into the darkness brandishing his sword but felt a blinding surge of energy and found himself in the Wildlands.

ELEMENT: FIRE
LIKES: FRESH BLOOD
DISLIKES: GARLIC GOULASH
WEAPON: SABRE

SPECIAL MOVE:
SOUL STEAL — Attacks enemy while restoring some of your own health.

FIGHTING FACTS

Renowned for his brutality, Vlad III of Wallachia killed a group of Turkish peace envoys by nailing their turbans to their heads. Their crime? Failing to raise their hats!

LEGENDARY

ALKAN
THE OTTOMAN SIPAHI

YEAR:
1480 AD

Racing towards Otranto Castle during the Ottoman invasion of Italy, Alkan was thrown from his horse when it was skewered by an enemy javelin. As arrows rained down, this reckless warrior continued on foot but was whisked to the Wildlands before he had a chance to behead a single priest!

ELEMENT: WATER
LIKES: RIDING BAREBACK
DISLIKES: SADDLE SORES
WEAPON: KILIJ SWORD
SPECIAL MOVE: FROZEN CRUNCH — Freeze and shatter your enemies with the elemental power of WATER.

FIGHTING FACTS

When the Ottomans raided Otranto in Southern Italy the Archbishop was beheaded and his companions were sawn in half.

RARE

133

AGE OF EXPLORATION

8. AGOOLIK

5. ORENDA

9. TEN BEARS

1. **CHAM** THE AZTEC JACKAL
1521 AD, MESOAMERICA

2. **KUKAN** THE MAYAN WARRIOR
1531 AD, MAYA, MESOAMERICA

3. **MANAWA** THE MAORI WARRIOR
1560 AD, AOTEARQA

4. **AKBAR** THE MUGHAL WARRIOR
1568 AD, MUGHAL EMPIRE

5. **ORENDA** THE IROQUOIS
1570 AD, KANONSIONNI

6. **NARO** THE SIAMESE WARRIOR
1584 AD, SIAM

7. **AMINA** THE ZAZZAU WARRIOR QUEEN
1594 AD, ZARIA

8. **AGOOLIK** THE INUIT WARRIOR
1680 AD, GREENLAND

9. **TEN BEARS** THE COMANCHE WARRIOR
1795 AD, FIRST NATION AMERICAS

10. **SHAKA** THE ZULU WARRIOR
1820 AD, ZULU KINGDOM

1. CHAM

2. KUKAN

7. AMINA

6. NARO

3. MANAWA

4. AKBAR

10. SHAKA

N
W   E
S

RARE

TITU
THE INCA WARRIOR

As the royal family's favourite bodyguard, life was good for Titu. But all that changed when he was framed for stealing an Incan talisman by a jealous high priest. Sentenced to death, this proud warrior was approaching Machu Picchu tied to a llama when he was summoned to the Wildlands.

ELEMENT: FIRE
LIKES: TREASURE
DISLIKES: ROPE BRIDGES
WEAPON: CLUB

SPECIAL MOVE:
POISON DART —
Poison any member
of the opposing team.

FIGHTING FACTS

Following his execution, the controversial thirteenth Inca Huascar's skull was transformed into a drinking jar ... by his own brother!

ZUMA
THE JAGUAR WARRIOR

Before entering the Wildlands, Zuma enraged fellow Jaguar Warriors with his reckless use of poison arrows. But they came in handy when he stumbled across a group of Conquistadors carrying a hoard of stolen Aztec gold. The Conquistadors are now mangrove mulch but the gold was never found.

ELEMENT: FIRE
LIKES: HUMAN SACRIFICE
DISLIKES: CONQUISTADORS
WEAPON: MACUAHUITL
SPECIAL MOVE: POISON –
Drain your enemy's energy slowly
as the fight progresses.

FIGHTING FACTS

As well as human sacrifice and gladiatorial combat, the Aztecs loved their macuahuitls – flesh-tearing wooden clubs embedded with razor sharp chunks of obsidian.

LEGENDARY

GONZALO
THE RODELEROS CONQUISTADOR

Rowing towards the Yucatan coast, Gonzalo was stunned to see countless Mayan warriors emerging from the mangroves waving their macuahuitls. Keeping them at bay with an oar, this brash, greedy Conquistador signalled his galleon to open fire but was summoned to the Wildlands just as its cannons exploded into life.

ELEMENT: FIRE
LIKES: DIVIDING AND CONQUERING
DISLIKES: HOME LIFE
WEAPON: TOLEDO SWORD
SPECIAL MOVE: ARMOUR BREAK –
Attack opponent and weaken their Armour.

FIGHTING FACTS
Defeated Inca Atahualpa offered Spanish Conquistador Francisco Pizarro a room filled with treasure in exchange for his life. Pizarro took the loot ... then executed him!

SUPER RARE

139

**YEAR:
1521 AD**

CHAM
THE AZTEC COYOTE

Summoned while battling the forces of Hernán Cortés during the fall of Tenochtitlan, Cham is a wily warrior who these days likes nothing more than taming the strange beasts of the Wildlands. Unfortunately these creatures often mistake him for one of their own, which can be painful!

ELEMENT: AIR
LIKES: ASTRONOMY
DISLIKES: FALSE GODS
WEAPON: MACUAHUITL
SPECIAL MOVE: POISON DART –
Poison any member of the opposing team.

FIGHTING FACTS

When Aztec warriors ran out of food they sometimes ate the flesh of their fallen foes. Yum!

LEGENDARY

140

KUKAN
THE MAYAN WARRIOR

Clambering down a jungle vine into a yawning limestone sinkhole, Kukan was certain he had finally escaped the traitors planning to sell him to Conquistadors. Unfortunately the silence was broken by a cutting noise and this illustrious warrior tumbled into the darkness towards a new life in the Wildlands.

ELEMENT: EARTH
LIKES: CHOCOLATE
DISLIKES: TREACHEROUS HIGH PRIESTS
WEAPON: CLUB
SPECIAL MOVE: POISON DART –
Poison any member of the opposing team.

FIGHTING FACTS

Mayans beat and hindered prisoners before forcing them to compete in ball games. Victors were then presented with the loser's head as a trophy.

SUPER RARE

141

MANAWA
THE MAORI WARRIOR

Performing a new haka alongside fellow raiders, Manawa was inches from an enemy warrior's face when he was unceremoniously head-butted. Waking up in a burning war canoe filled with dead bodies, he wondered if his haka had invoked the wrong gods, when suddenly he was summoned to the Wildlands.

ELEMENT: WATER
LIKES: WAR HAKAS
DISLIKES: SHARK TEETH
WEAPON: PATU
SPECIAL MOVE: WATER BOOST —
Temporarily increase WATER damage inflicted by all team members.

FIGHTING FACTS

Some Maori warriors ate enemies killed in battle, and prisoners often had their legs broken in order to prevent escape before being consumed. Mmm!

LEGENDARY

AKBAR
THE MUGHAL WARRIOR

YEAR: 1568 AD

Separated from his fellow Mughals during the conquest of Rajputana, Akbar was crawling through cobra-infested paddy fields when he felt himself being dragged face-first into the sodden ground. Choking on earth and rice, this valiant warrior finally surfaced from the mire, only to find himself in the Wildlands.

ELEMENT: AIR
LIKES: ELABORATE COINS
DISLIKES: RICE
WEAPON: TALWAR

SPECIAL MOVE:
ROLLING THUNDER —
Strikes three random opponents.

FIGHTING FACTS

To increase momentum the blade of the talwar sword widened near the tip, allowing warriors to amputate limbs and decapitate enemies with a single blow.

COMMON

YEAR:
1570 AD

ORENDA
THE MOHAWK WARRIOR

Double-crossed during a fur exchange near the Mohawk River, Orenda was stalking the Algonquians who had betrayed him when his tomahawk began to glow. Staring at the blade, this fierce warrior was suddenly swathed in blue light and summoned to the Wildlands before he had a chance to react.

ELEMENT:	AIR	**SPECIAL MOVE:**
LIKES:	KAYAKING	SURPRISE — Performs
DISLIKES:	CARIBOU STEW	a randomly selected
WEAPON:	TOMAHAWK	Special Move.

FIGHTING FACTS

Many tomahawks featured a pipe bowl opposite the blade and a hollow handle to allow for smoking.

LEGENDARY

McCABE
THE GALLOWGLASS MERCENARY

Summoned to the Wildlands after kidnapping the son of a prominent landowner, McCabe now wonders what became of the lad because his conscience finally kicked in and he had already decided to release him without collecting his usual ransom of nine sheep and a barrel of ale.

ELEMENT: EARTH
LIKES: MONEY FOR NOTHING
DISLIKES: BENEVOLENCE
WEAPON: SPARTH AXE
SPECIAL MOVE: ARMOUR BREAK — Attack opponent and weaken their Armour.

FIGHTING FACTS

Gallowglasses were elite mercenary warriors who fought for various European armies and often served as personal bodyguards to military leaders.

LEGENDARY

KURO
THE MIDNIGHT NINJA

Master of stealth, Kuro has refused to remove his black garb ever since he arrived in the Wildlands. This has led to rumours that he is the mysterious Ninja warrior who was last spotted scaling Azuchi Castle shortly before an assassination attempt on a notorious Japanese warlord.

ELEMENT: AIR
LIKES: ESPIONAGE
DISLIKES: LOUD NOISES
WEAPON: CHOKUTŌ
SPECIAL MOVE: STEALTH STRIKE –
Attack all enemies without tagging into the fight.

FIGHTING FACTS

Ninja sometimes used blowguns (fukiya) to temporarily disable targets with blinding powder made from crushed glass, pepper and iron filings.

LEGENDARY

NARO
THE SIAMESE WARRIOR

YEAR: 1584 AD

After years of devoted service, Naro's loyalty crumbled when he was overlooked for promotion. He led a brutal rebellion against his kingdom before the Wildlands called him.

ELEMENT: FIRE
LIKES: SHARPENED TUSKS
DISLIKES: BEING OVERLOOKED FOR PROMOTION
WEAPON: DHA
SPECIAL MOVE: THUNDER STRIKE —
Electrocute enemies with the power of lightning.

FIGHTING FACTS

Southeast Asian troops would thwart war elephants with massed crossbow fire and hidden pits filled with huge spikes.

RARE

147

AMINA
THE ZAZZAU WARRIOR QUEEN

Leading her troops into battle just outside Atagara, Amina was at the pinnacle of her power, having conquered countless territories across Nigeria and beyond. But fate intervened when this fierce warrior queen was summoned to the Wildlands while pummelling an enemy chief with a gigantic coconut shell.

ELEMENT: AIR
LIKES: KOLA NUTS
DISLIKES: MARRIAGE
WEAPON: SWORD
SPECIAL MOVE: POISON —
Drain enemies slowly with Poison.

FIGHTING FACTS

According to legend, Zazzau warrior queen Amina took vanquished foes as temporary husbands after every battle, but would condemn them to death in the morning.

LEGENDARY

KIBI
THE DANI CHIEF

Returning home to his wives following a successful headhunting trip near the Papuan coast, Kibi spotted a wizened old man beckoning him towards a hollow tree trunk. Eager to add to his head collection, this ferocious chief moved to attack but was summoned to the Wildlands in a blue flash.

ELEMENT: WATER
LIKES: MUDDY MASKS
DISLIKES: BURNT BOAR
WEAPON: CLUB

SPECIAL MOVE:
POISON DART — Poison any member of the opposing team.

FIGHTING FACTS

If a Dani warrior died, his female relatives would cut off a fingertip, a tradition that lives on today.

LEGENDARY

AGOOLIK
THE INUIT WARRIOR

Returning from a hunting trip aboard his trusty dog sled, Agoolik was ambushed by rival tribesmen who made off with his precious hoard of walrus teeth. Battered and stranded, this quick-witted warrior took shelter in an abandoned igloo, but when he emerged at dawn he was lost in the Wildlands.

ELEMENT: WATER
LIKES: HIS HUSKIES
DISLIKES: POLAR BEAR LIVER
WEAPON: STONE AXE

SPECIAL MOVE: PHANTOM SHIELD — Boosts the Armour strength of all team members.

FIGHTING FACTS

Most Inuit weapons were designed for hunting and butchering, and their serrated blades were perfect for tearing and mauling rather than slicing and puncturing. Ouch!

LEGENDARY

KADAM
THE MARATHA WARRIOR

Pursued by a raging tiger along the banks of the Savitri River, Kadam found himself trapped, teetering on the edge of a massive waterfall. Deciding to face the beast, this mighty warrior lashed out with his shield but toppled backwards into the cascading water before surfacing in the Wildlands.

ELEMENT: FIRE
LIKES: A TIDY BEARD
DISLIKES: CATS
WEAPON: KHANDA
SPECIAL MOVE: INFERNO –
Burn enemies with the elemental power of FIRE.

FIGHTING FACTS

Having been captured by the enemy, Sambhaji, founder of the Maratha Empire, was paraded around in clown's clothes before being chopped to pieces.

SUPER RARE

AMANAR
THE TUAREG TRIBESMAN

Resting during an epic trek across the Sahara, Amanar was staring at the stars when he heard whispering. Spotting countless bandits behind a distant dune, this irrepressible warrior attempted to lead his camels to safety, but was summoned to the Wildlands before he could even sharpen his takoba.

ELEMENT: WATER
LIKES: MINT TEA
DISLIKES: TOUCHING IRON
WEAPON: TAKOBA
SPECIAL MOVE: PHANTOM STRIKE —
Inflicts high physical damage to all enemies.

FIGHTING FACTS

The Tuareg have an aversion to touching iron so their deadly double-edge swords feature a hilt that is fully covered, often in leather, brass or silver.

LEGENDARY

TEN BEARS
THE COMANCHE WARRIOR

This ferocious warrior has been wreaking havoc in the Wildlands ever since he was summoned during a raid on a Texan settlement. An expert horseman, Ten Bears is renowned for his ability to tame any beast. But his main talent is his ability to hurl his axe with painful accuracy.

ELEMENT: AIR
LIKES: FERAL HORSES
DISLIKES: UNTANGLING HAIR BRAIDS
WEAPON: AXE

SPECIAL MOVE:
VENGEANCE –
Attack power rises
as health reduces.

FIGHTING FACTS

The Comanche were specialists in pain, sometimes staking out naked captives over beds of red ants.

153

ANTIKO
THE IGOROT WARRIOR

Summoned to the Wildands while guarding a Kalingan rice field after a spate of enemy raids, Antiko is known for his fast, ferocious fighting style and his ability to weave sturdy baskets, which he uses to store his ever-increasing collection of severed heads and limbs.

ELEMENT:	FIRE	**SPECIAL MOVE:**
LIKES:	LOOM WEAVING	REGENERATION —
DISLIKES:	PIERCINGS	Gradually restores health to
WEAPON:	HEAD AXE	all team members.

FIGHTING FACTS

When an Igorot warrior hunted his first enemy head, he was entitled to get a distinctive head-taker's tattoo.

RARE

155

RARE

156

SHAKA
THE ZULU WARRIOR

A formidable warrior, Shaka was returning home from an initiation ceremony when he noticed what looked like a female hand beckoning him through a waterfall. Baffled but curious, he jumped across some rocks and plunged through the curtain of cascading water, only to find himself trapped in the Wildlands.

ELEMENT: EARTH
LIKES: DISTANT DRUMS
DISLIKES: MOSQUITOES
WEAPON: IKLWA

SPECIAL MOVE:
SURPRISE – Performs a randomly selected Special Move.

FIGHTING FACTS

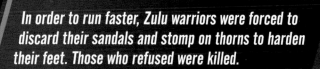
In order to run faster, Zulu warriors were forced to discard their sandals and stomp on thorns to harden their feet. Those who refused were killed.

157

CROCKETT
THE FEARSOME FRONTIERSMAN

Summoned to the Wildlands while frantically defending the Alamo from Mexican troops, Crockett often wonders what became of his beloved Texas, because the last thing he remembers from that fateful day is yanking his knife from its sheath, having realized he was surrounded and plum outta ammo.

ELEMENT: WATER
LIKES: SKINNING BEARS
DISLIKES: PESKY VARMINTS
WEAPON: HUNTING KNIFE
SPECIAL MOVE: SWITCH STRIKE —
Target specific members of
opposing teams.

FIGHTING FACTS

With no time to reload, Davy Crockett is said to have died defending the Alamo with just a small knife and the butt of his trusty musket.

LEGENDARY

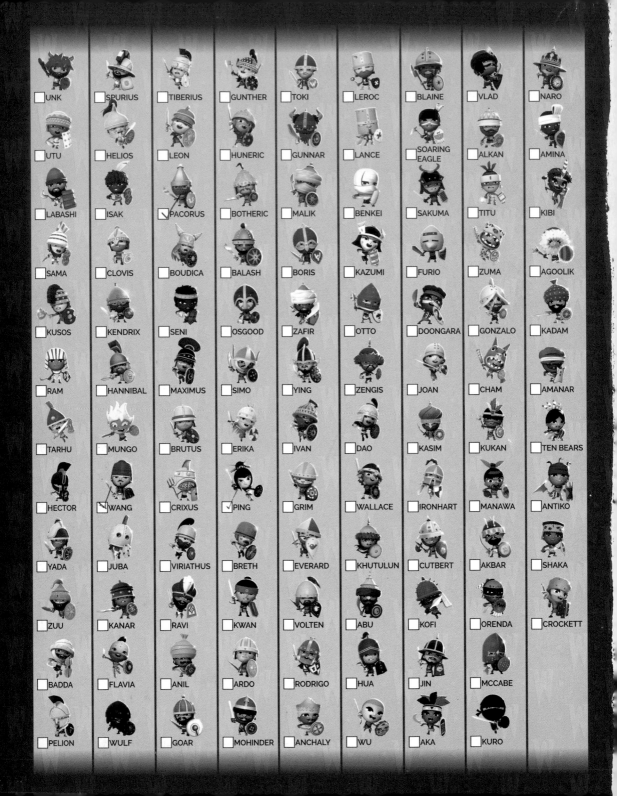

☐ UNK	☐ SPURIUS	☐ TIBERIUS	☐ GUNTHER	☐ TOKI	☐ LEROC	☐ BLAINE	☐ VLAD	☐ NARO
☐ UTU	☐ HELIOS	☐ LEON	☐ HUNERIC	☐ GUNNAR	☐ LANCE	☐ SOARING EAGLE	☐ ALKAN	☐ AMINA
☐ LABASHI	☐ ISAK	☑ PACORUS	☐ BOTHERIC	☐ MALIK	☐ BENKEI	☐ SAKUMA	☐ TITU	☐ KIBI
☐ SAMA	☐ CLOVIS	☐ BOUDICA	☐ BALASH	☐ BORIS	☐ KAZUMI	☐ FURIO	☐ ZUMA	☐ AGOOLIK
☐ KUSOS	☐ KENDRIX	☐ SENI	☐ OSGOOD	☐ ZAFIR	☐ OTTO	☐ DOONGARA	☐ GONZALO	☐ KADAM
☐ RAM	☐ HANNIBAL	☐ MAXIMUS	☐ SIMO	☐ YING	☐ ZENGIS	☐ JOAN	☐ CHAM	☐ AMANAR
☐ TARHU	☐ MUNGO	☐ BRUTUS	☐ ERIKA	☐ IVAN	☐ DAO	☐ KASIM	☐ KUKAN	☐ TEN BEARS
☐ HECTOR	☑ WANG	☐ CRIXUS	☑ PING	☐ GRIM	☐ WALLACE	☐ IRONHART	☐ MANAWA	☐ ANTIKO
☐ YADA	☐ JUBA	☐ VIRIATHUS	☐ BRETH	☐ EVERARD	☐ KHUTULUN	☐ CUTBERT	☐ AKBAR	☐ SHAKA
☐ ZUU	☐ KANAR	☐ RAVI	☐ KWAN	☐ VOLTEN	☐ ABU	☐ KOFI	☐ ORENDA	☐ CROCKETT
☐ BADDA	☐ FLAVIA	☐ ANIL	☐ ARDO	☐ RODRIGO	☐ HUA	☐ JIN	☐ MCCABE	
☐ PELION	☐ WULF	☐ GOAR	☐ MOHINDER	☐ ANCHALY	☐ WU	☐ AKA	☐ KURO